ROAD PIRATES

Photographs by Marc Hauser

Text by Judy Robb

CHICAGO
REVIEW
PRESS

*To my dad,
who started me on the road to photography
and gave me my first camera*

Hauser, Marc
    Road pirates: photographs/by Marc Hauser; text by Judy Robb.
    p. cm.
    ISBN 1-55652-136-7:
    1. Motorcyclists—Portraits.   2. Motorcyclists—Social life and customs.   I. Robb, Judy.   II. Title.
TR681.M69H38   1991
779'.2'092—dc20

Cover and interior design: Fran Lee

Copyright © 1991 by Marc Hauser

All rights reserved
First Edition
Published by Chicago Review Press, Incorporated
814 North Franklin Street, Chicago, Illinois, 60610

1   2   3   4   5   6   7   8   9   10

ISBN 1-55652-136-7
Printed in the United States of America

ACKNOWLEDGMENTS

We would like to thank Scott Shigley and Ron Gordon Photo; Carol Cheeseman; John McArthur; Corinne Tabor; and Marlene and Offie's Tap, Main Street, Huntley.

*"FTW: Fuck The World.
I'm my own person. I do what I want.
Nobody puts chains on me."*
—Anonymous Biker

INTRODUCTION

I discovered Offie's Tap on a Sunday afternoon while driving through a small northern Illinois town looking for a tavern where I could have a beer. It was one of those warm January days, and I saw some Harleys parked on the corner outside the bar. Marlene was tending bar, I consumed many beers, met the great people that hang out there, and really enjoyed myself. I became an Offie's Sunday afternoon regular. I met bikers from all over the area, as Offie's Tap is their meeting place. I found out about other biker hangouts and events. Many of the people represented in this book have become very close friends. When you're a biker you're a member of a large family, one that is recognized wherever you go. Bikers can be some of the most caring people on earth with the biggest hearts. Even at Sturgis, the Black Hills Motor Classic, where there may have been six hundred thousand bikers in attendance for the fiftieth anniversary, the brotherhood is there. Bikers from all over the world, with varying backgrounds, stories, and affiliations, congregate at Sturgis. Everyone shares in the common bond in his or her own way and gets along, and if there are skirmishes it is usually a private matter, and those not involved are respected and left alone.

In the time I have spent with bikers I've gained a perspective and feeling about people that I will carry with me always. Bikers will do anything to help out a friend or someone in need, and when you spend time living the life with them, you probably will understand.

—Judy Robb

RICK

"The first bike I got was a Honda. I was seventeen. I had to use it to go to school. It had no second gear. I had to go from first to third. I finally blew it up at the Clark gas station where I was pumpin' gas, doin' wheelies for the bigger guys. I had it about a year. Then it was later that I got a 350 Honda.

And I wanted to get a 750 but they were too much money. And then I went to a Sportster. I was probably about twenty-two or twenty-three. Those Sportster years. I bought it used from a friend of mine. I put money into it and fixed it up. Chains and tires and cleaned it up and painted it, shit like that. Nothing major—all on a budget. And then I got myself a '76 Electra Glide in '78 or '79, on a shady deal. And I rode that for two years. That was the first bike I took to Sturgis. Then I got my '62. I've been takin' it to Sturgis since then, every year. This was my tenth year and I really like the old girl, but I want a new one."

ON HARLEYS

"There's no other bike like a Harley. Without gettin' too cliche, until you've ridden on a Harley, you haven't ridden a motorcycle. The others are just copies, toys, faint expressions. It's the low-end torque.

RICK

1962 Harley-Davidson Duo Glide

It's the sound of the bike. It's the macho image that it's had all these years. It just feels good. A certain sense of accomplishment. Because the older the Harley is, the more adjustments need to be made. Harleys never break down; they just need more adjustments. And for a guy to keep it well adjusted enough to make a long trip is kind of a feather in his hat. A badge of honor.

"The first few years I came to Sturgis it was always with the guys. It was pretty good. Now I've gotten to appreciate female company. For the obvious reasons that they're better to look at and they make better breakfasts. But they have their drawbacks, too."

DINO & MIKE

Mike rides an '88 FLHS—a stripped down full dresser, no radio or faring. Dino rides what he calls the Dinosaur—a '73 shovelhead and a '57 hardtail. It's got a '47 springer front end. Sometimes he changes it with a '68 Hydraglide, when he gets tired of riding one or the other. Now it has ape hangers.

Mike's married to Judy, and they ride all over the country together. Dino says he's faithful to no one; that he does what he wants to with "no ties to nobody." Neither Dino nor Mike likes riding somewhere in a large group. You never end up doing what you want to do. Dino says, "It's like being with twenty disoriented fucks. They spend half their time gettin' their bikes ready or at least gettin' on their bikes and gettin' 'em fuckin' started."

Mike feels the same way: "There's too many of 'em that are very inexperienced riders. Now that Harley-Davidson is a big thing it's in to own a Harley. You got a lot of guys that have bought Harleys and have become HOG members; they're like MEGATS saying 'God, he's goin' forty-five.' Cuz they're scared to go fast."

Dino is originally from LA, and Mike lived in Florida for a long time. Both of them have seen a lot of shit go down and have been involved in it themselves. They seem wise in their years and pretty mellow. Common sense rules now. Their viewpoints are consistent and based on tried and true logic.

Dino and Mike are pretty vehement in their feelings toward bikers as a whole, patriotism, and the 1%ers.

Mike: "To me, the average American doesn't realize where bikers are really coming from and what they're really like. We are very, very patriotic, America-loving people. Many of us are Vietnam veterans. I can't really describe how patriotic bikers are and really love America. They're good people and people just don't understand them. That's what it boils down to. They can't look past the long hair and the movie image. They pull into town, tear the town apart, and rape the women, kill the babies, rape some of the men.

"I think a lot of the 1%er people are good people. One percent of society, the AMA considered these outlaw people to be one percent of the motorcycling public. The bad-image people, according to the AMA.

Dino: "Thousands of 1%ers and their satellite groups, a lot of them are good people. I would say 10 percent maybe at the max are bad people who maybe live the life-style of 'we don't give a fuck what rules are, we don't give a fuck what laws say, we do what we

want, when we want; and if we get busted we can handle it, we can do the time.' But even so it's a very small percentage of even 1%ers that are the movie image of the vicious biker. They're the ones who had no regard for the law. They wrote their own laws. They did and they came and they went as they pleased, and they didn't care about nothing else but their own needs. A 1%er is out of society's so-called way to act. Walk up to a woman and drag her into an alley because she looks good. It's against society's rules. That stuff happens, it still happens. I've lived side by side with 1%ers and a lot of them have become friends of mine. They are looked down upon cuz they can't abide by society's rules, but society's rules are fucked anyway. It's like a bond. You know who you can depend upon in any group situation. If anything comes down to where they need to depend on each other, they will depend on each other—it's there. They're always there for each other no matter how shitty the times are."

SCOOTER TRAMPS, 1%ERS, STURGIS & CLUBS

The quotes in this story were gathered from bikers all over the U.S.A. They don't necessarily represent the opinions of those shown in the photographs, and for the most part the sources will remain anonymous.

There's a lot of different kinds of bikers. From the lone wolf who only answers to himself, to the club member responsible to everyone his patch represents. Bikers, Harley guys especially, tend to look alike—beards, black T-shirts, and vests. Yet they all do something in their appearance to make themselves unique, whether it's a patch,  a pin, or some way of making their bike special. A code name may have a particular meaning, with a story behind it that means a lot to the person carrying it. Whatever it is, a biker's friend or brother knows what it is and the history behind it. Each name has a meaning, and if you show an interest that's genuine, they'll tell you the story and then maybe you'll be a brother, too.

The term scooter tramp has a history, too. There aren't many true scooter tramps around anymore. The American Motorcycle Association (AMA) in the middle sixties made a statement that 99 percent of the motorcyclists in this country were good, honest, hardworking, god-fearing, law abiding citizens; it's only 1 percent that creates the problems. To the AMA, only 1 percent that in their opinion were trash and tramps. Hence, the bikers said, if you're going to call us tramps, we're tramps. The term for a motorcycle has always been scooter. You don't hear it much anymore, but back in the sixties and seventies, if you rode a bike, it was a scooter. Definitely, they're not scooters, but that's the term that was used. The term scooter tramp is a label by society.

"If we're tramps, we're tramps. That's the life we lead. We don't ride the rails, we ride the roads and we ride them on two wheels."

A guy in Sturgis said, *"You don't have to be black to be a nigger. Kinda like labeling theory. A stereotype. There's always a man underneath the vest. Or a woman. A person. Any label has what you identify it with. A statement of camaraderie in some man's mind. It might mean something derogatory to others. It's the common bond of brotherhood. We all like the common bond of*

HOME BREW

riding. People see the black leather and T-shirt and they hassle me. They don't even know what I do or what I have."

It seems that bikers tend to dress alike for this common bond. One guy may work forty hours in a factory. Another may own his or her own business. But they look the same.  Society sees the way they dress and immediately labels them as bad, trouble waiting to happen.

"The image had already been planted in the fifties of guys who rode motorcycles, especially if you rode Harleys, or Enfields, or Indians, or Triumphs, or BSAs. You were bad. Especially the image if you wore a black leather jacket, and of course everybody that rode at that time generally wore the traditional uniform. Jeans, a jacket, white T-shirt—like the old movies had, as nobody had turned to black yet, and your boots. That was just the accepted thing that you wore.

"So at that time you didn't want to get caught riding a motorcycle. You'd ride with your buddies, but you did not ride

T-BONE

a motorcycle to pick up a girl or go to a family outing, cuz immediately the family thought you were up to no good. And so people that were tramps were scooter tramps. And a lot of them liked the image. They liked the freedom they got. And as more and more people rode, and more and more were ostracized by the community, the more of them had a tendency to band together. And the scooter tramp name just stayed."

The scooter tramp image and the banding together played a major role in the formation and popularity of clubs. Because people would ride together, it seemed they would become a target for the authorities to check up on and see what they were doing. The image formed, and a lot of people liked the image. B movies did a lot to perpetuate it. These movies would oftentimes portray real events, but would glamorize them and make them more than they really were. But they have to have that image. However, it seems that the image is waning, and in larger cities, street gangs are much more prevalent than bike clubs. Even when you see clubs together, people tend to not be afraid of them anymore. The violence in society has probably had something to do with that.

OUCH

But in the last two or three years there has been a growth in the sixties image of what a bike gang is. It may be their last hurrah, their last chance to blow off steam and make themselves noticed. Maybe it will last forever, but maybe it's going to die. It's the opinion  of a lot of bikers that the media has played a major role in the image of what a motorcyclist is. Most say the media only shows biker news when they screw up. This is what the newspapers and television tend to emphasize, and what you read in the paper is what people are going to believe.

Bikers as a whole are good people. A lot of the clubs have Christmas parties for underprivileged kids every year. The kids whose family can't afford to buy them toys. That's how the annual Toy Run got started. In Chicago, it's held every December, with two to five thousand bikers, not just clubbers but all different kinds of bikers showing up, each with a toy for a child. If it were held earlier in the season, more people would probably participate. Baltimore has their Toy Run in October, and have participation of

DINO

about eighty thousand people. But the bikers don't really get any publicity out of it.

"These bikers don't have to do this. They want to. They don't get anything out of it cuz the news media won't give them shit. You get the bad publicity. More toys are given by bikers at Christmas time than any other group. And that's all across the country. And the media never shows the families. They never show the family life that some of these bikers have. And some of them have a pretty damn good family life. As wild and as free as most of the bikers are, their contention of the way things have to be in the family, there's a high percentage that stay real tight to the family. These guys may not be off the street, but you better believe their kids are."

M. C. STARS

The family feeling is an important thing to bikers. Whether it's their own flesh and blood, or good friends. This is how the annual Sturgis Black Hills Motor Classic became so popular. It began only as a small get-together in 1938. Pappy Howell got together with some of his war buddies. Probably twelve people. This small group would get together and race. Because they were friends from the war, they were from all over the country. Each year they'd bring their friends and it just grew. It was just a weekend. This year Sturgis celebrated its fiftieth anniversary. No one knows for sure how many were there, maybe three hundred thousand. But for a town with a population of only thirty-five hundred, that's a lot of bikers.

Sturgis has turned into a commercial entity. Ten years ago it was a lot less commercial. It was more about bikes, with shows and races. More people show up every year, because they like the brotherhood and meeting the people from all over the world that feel the same way they do. You make connections and you make friends.

BRAD

"Sturgis is a oneness. People go to express their uniqueness. To show off the totally individual expression of each person. To some guys, their jacket is more important than their coat or their bike's more important than their old lady or how it looks makes more of a statement than how it runs. Everybody's into their own thing. And it's great. It's a mecca for motorcyclists. For Harley-Davidson riders."

ZIGGY

The actual attendance at Sturgis is probably not known. Fifteen to twenty percent are usually not counted, such as people that are running, have had trouble with the law, or people that just show up and crash with friends and don't want to pay for a campsite. A lot of people never even go into the town of Sturgis itself, either because they are traveling around the area, want to avoid the crowds, or want to avoid the federal agents that are everywhere during Sturgis, and they don't want to be seen. These are the people that don't sign their name anywhere. They don't want anyone to know who they are or where they are staying. The clubs gather at Sturgis and most of them have their own property to camp on as a group. Not many people know where these camps are. The clubs go to Sturgis to party, show their colors, and show their force. It's see and be seen. But there usually isn't any hassle, unless there's a vendetta between clubs that has to be settled. Everyone is on best behavior. Sturgis is considered a neutral ground now, but in 1982, it really went to hell. A lot of people talk about '82, and how wild it was.

GEORGE

"Clubs were there in force. One club was on a national run, and showed up in pretty good force. Another club tried to get to the campground where this club was partying. The cops wouldn't let them go in. They stopped them on the highway and told them you can't go. One of them shoved a cop. Instantaneously he was on the ground with a nightstick on his throat. A lot of them were getting off their bikes and the cops told 'em 'don't move' and these club guys realized that all of the cops had rifles or shotguns. They were told they were held back because of bad blood between them and the other club."

There are a lot of really decent guys that are members of clubs. But a lot of them have insecurities about themselves, so that may be one reason they ride within a club. The club becomes the family. And it's a real strong family to these guys. But after awhile, the families fight amongst themselves and the clubs fight amongst themselves.

JACK LOVE

"There are clubmembers that will steal other clubmembers' bikes. There are clubmembers that all they do is steal bikes, and they'll do it together and then another club member that helped them steal the bikes will steal them away from their own club member. Unfortunately they get caught in their own shit and it makes them look bad. But there are a lot of guys in clubs that are not up to shit and no good. There's a lot of them that are really straight people."

It seems that the power these clubs generate and the money they earn is in the way of drug trafficking. It's big money, and when it comes to the clubs, as they grow, their territories overlap, creating conflict between the different clubs.

BEAR

"There are a lot of club guys that don't even do drugs. But all the clubs today are into drugs. Either using, selling, distributing, or whatever. All of them. There isn't a club today that isn't into drugs in some way. And most of them are in the business end of it. It's become a business that they can't pass up. They travel by motorcycle long distances. Sometimes on the excuse of runs. Oddly enough, even the little clubs are doing it now. Not just the established 1%er clubs, but even the little clubs runnin' around on their Ninjas and stuff like that. And they're into it. Not maybe, they are drug pushers."

Because of the possibility that clubs may be involved in drugs, many bikers prefer to be their own entity.

"If you take thirty or forty dudes and you're all wearin' the same colors and one of 'em happens to do some acid or somethin' and kill somebody or somethin' like that and you're wearin' that patch on your jacket, you're representin' some asshole. Sorta like makes ya responsible. They see the patch on your back, you know, this gang did it or that gang did it. And if you're wearin' those colors, it's sorta like you did it. That's why I don't wear no colors, no patch."

KEVIN

Some bikers are simply motorcycle enthusiasts, traveling bikers that just want to ride for the sake of a vacation, and some are 1%ers that don't want any affiliation with a negative image. Some bikers just like to put on miles. They like to see things and go places. They are unique in that they don't go for patches and being a clubber. They just like to get up and go and see things in a laid-back atmosphere. Club guys generally like to travel in packs.

"Some of these club guys, they just need somebody to tell them what to do. They're that insecure in their own ability to do something by themselves so they need the format of a club, an officer, a president—someone else making all the decisions for them. And that's a certain kind of person, too. There's some guys in prison who like being in prison because everything's structured for them. There's guys in the army. They like the army. Being  *an outlaw biker I think combines a lot of things. There's a lot of pluses and minuses just like everything. It all gets weighed out in*

LITTLE G.

the end. There's room for everybody. But there's too many people hung up on playin' a role for all bikers to come together. Acting out some bullshit they saw on TV. A lot of bikers get down on the public for giving us that stereotypical movie/TV image, but there's so many assholes perpetuating that image just by the way they act that you can see where these people still have that idea. Everybody can do their own thing. You just have to watch out where you are and who you're with, that's all."

There are bikers that run with clubs but are not members. They like to hang out with them, but either don't want to have to go on every run that's mandatory or just don't want to wear any colors. Yet a lot of them say being in a club has its appealing side.

"Club guys are alright. A bunch of good guys. It all depends what kind of mood they're in. Depending on what they're coming back from. They can tear some shit up if they want to. They handle their stuff the way they want to handle it. Being in a club is a lot of fun. I've been in about four different clubs already. It can be a gas. The parties are nice. It's just too heavy for me right now. I've had a bunch of gun beefs and stuff like that. That's a reason I don't join

SPIDER

clubs. If you're in a club, you're bound to get in some fuckin' trouble with the law, more than likely. And I think I've stretched my limits as far as I could."

As one guy put it, bikers are the "salt of the earth." When you're on the road, you're thinking your own thoughts, regardless of who you are or whether or not you're in a club. That's why a gathering like Sturgis is great. It brings all the different kinds of motorcycle enthusiasts together. They all have one common bond. The bike and the road. It doesn't matter what kind of bike you ride. The brotherhood is the same. If all the bikers—the outlaw bikers and all the other people that ride—would come together and work out their problems, bikers would become a powerful entity.

"It used to be in the late sixties, no matter who you saw or what you were ridin', you always waved. There was a certain camaraderie. I had a little 250 Triumph. There was still the certain feeling of oneness. Now it's 'my dog's better than your dog, or my coke's better than your coke, or my bike's better than your bike.' It used to be that everybody rode together. You'd go out for a ride on a Sunday, and by the end of the day you'd be traveling in a group, a group of

all different kinds of bikes. Now there's all this shit, 'fuck the jap bikes, American is best.' Now you see it at Sturgis. It seems like there's no real brotherhood there."

If there is a brotherhood, maybe bikers should just cut the crap and discover that it isn't just among the clubs or the kind of bike you ride, but among all the people that ride. When a club guy at Sturgis was once asked to introduce his friend he summed it all up by saying "that's not my friend, that's my brother."

AL

"I'm just a lone biker. Stay out of trouble and keep my cools."

AL

JIM

PIRATE

"I love bikin'. I'll never stop lovin' it. I've been bikin' for about twenty years. Ya just get on it and go to it. It's a lot of fun. As long as you don't get cracked up over it. I've always been drivin' 'em. All my life. As soon as I've been able to crawl up on one, I've been diggin' 'em. I hardly ever stay bikeless. I always got a bike. I ride in the ice, the snow, the sleet, and the rain. It doesn't matter to me, man. I hook up with different clubs here and there. Partners. Just runnin' around wolf packin'. Usually bar hoppin' and stuff like that. But I'd rather be the lone ranger."

PIRATE

BIRDMAN

Birdman is a tattoo artist and a certified pastry chef. He has decorated wedding cakes, ripped people off all over the U.S.A., and spent time in the pokey. The black and white tattoos on his arms and chest are homemade. Birdman has a special feeling for the symbol of the American eagle. Birdman was born in Arkansas in the back of a pickup truck. His parents were moonshiners. He'd like to see his picture hanging up on the walls of women's prisons all over the country. He says he wants to be famous.

BIRDMAN

OLD MAN LARRY

TWO DOGS
"A woman's place is on the back of the bike."

TWO DOGS

CHUCK

HARLEY DRAGS
HAVANA, ILLINOIS

I rode on the back of Ralph's FLH Police Special to the Harley Drags in Havana, Illinois. Chuck and his chick followed in a pickup truck carrying a '67 Triumph chopper. They were planning on entering the chopper in the bike show at the drags, but the bike would never start so they didn't enter it. It was a week after Sturgis. Chuck's bike had blown up on the way home from that trip and was now in a barn somewhere in Minnesota. The back of the truck was loaded with camping gear, beer, and ice. Ralph's bike had a pair of cheap bikini briefs hanging on the handle bars. He said some "bimbo" had taken them off while riding on the back the night before.

We had to stop a couple of times along the way to make adjustments in the truck's gas line and guzzle a couple of beers. At one point we hit a torrential downpour of rain. I could feel the front tire of the bike slip on the wet pavement every now and then, and cold adrenaline would surge through my body. The climate suddenly changed to sunny, hot, and muggy so we stopped to drink another beer.

We rolled into Havana late in the afternoon. The racetrack was

on the outskirts of town surrounded by corn, soybean, and alfalfa fields. We rode down a bumpy dirt road and stopped at the gate to pay our weekend fee. The guy taking the money put an orange plastic band on each of our wrists. We continued up a hill to a camping area that overlooked the track. We set up our tents on a freshly mowed pasture filled with prickly cactuses. The sun was going down as we drank a few more beers.

A van with a sofa next to it was parked in the nearby campsite. There were a couple of guys, one of their old ladies, and some children; they all spoke with a southern Illinois hillbilly drawl. Ralph and Chuck dug a pit for a bonfire and our neighbors dragged their sofa over to it. The sounds from the campers surrounding us became more intense as the afternoon's beer consumption kicked in.

Chuck's chick put on a tube top that said "I'm not your fuckin baby." She had a dog collar made of chain hanging around her neck that had a leash clipped to it. Chuck and Ralph attached their keys to the collar. There was a bracelet and ring held together by three chains on one of her hands, with an eagle emblem holding the chains together.

We went down to the main grounds below the racetrack and

devoured some hotdogs at the only concession stand. There was a large tent that contained the bike show and vendors selling clothing, leather goods, jewelry, and used motorcycle parts. There was a small stage with a bar band in tight leather pants and bouffant hairdos playing metal covers. Behind the crowd were cattle-watering containers made of galvanized steel filled with melting ice and cans of beer you could buy for a buck. We grabbed a few and walked to the opposite end of the vendors' strip to Dragon's tattoo trailer.

Surrounding it were guys in beat-up sleeveless jean jackets, wearing club patches that were unfamiliar to me. One guy was looking for a lost contact lens in the grass. Dragon came across as rough and surly, like he had seen it all. Two folding tables leaning against the trailer supported photo album–type books filled with black and white tattoo imagery. There were a couple of young guys flipping the pages, nervously trying to make a decision. Ralph picked out a flaming skull image he wanted tattooed on either side of a grim reaper already tattooed on his upper left arm. While we were waiting I asked some of the guys standing around what some of their patches meant. They grumbled something I could not understand. Ralph told me women could not understand normal thinking. I could sense my questions were not appreciated, and Dragon asked him how he knew me. Dragon and Ralph went into the trailer. I followed and watched for a few minutes, Dragon again asked Ralph where he found me, and I left to buy some beers. Dragon said I was making him nervous.

I wandered around the band area and bought some cans of warm Old Style. There was a tit contest and the women were showing their stuff. Some of them had elaborate tattoos on their breasts. The women for the most part were slender, wearing T-shirts that were roughly trimmed to expose more flesh. I went back to the trailer and Dragon was almost finished with Ralph's flaming skulls. I was told about the grim reaper and how you have to face it because it's always around. Ralph said Indians aren't afraid of dying and that I should know that from my history. We made our way back to the campsite to find the hillbillies feeling pretty high and partying around the campfire. They pulled out a purple bong and passed it around. The children were looking tired and limp. The mother sat on the couch looking catatonic. There were campfires with groups like this one all around, about fifty feet apart from each other. You could hear the murmur of the respective conversations floating from campsite to campsite. The parties went on for hours. The conversations dwindled and the remainder of the evening was silent, broken up only by the fire popping.

Most everyone was holding a can of beer and staring into the fire. I finally crawled off to the tent and passed out, exhausted from the day's events and revelry.

I woke up at dawn on a wet sleeping bag. Some guy was starting up his Sportster, and through the tent wall it sounded like it was only a foot away. I stumbled out of the tent and made my way to the women's latrine, a wooden building that enclosed six outhouse-like holes in a circle. There were no lights and no mirrors. I had to rely on the rearview mirror of the truck to adjust my smeared mascara. There weren't many people up at this hour, so I wandered around for awhile and drank a warm beer. Later we drove into Havana to a family-type restaurant for a huge breakfast buffet.

By the time we got back I was ready for a nap, but the activities down at the drag strip were in full swing. Most everyone looked a little rough around the edges from the night before. I managed to get down on the track to the pit area to see the drag bikes take off while I breathed the burning nitro fuel.

We got back on the road to Chicago pretty early in the day. It was a beautiful sunny day and I was content to get lost in my thoughts sitting on the back seat of the bike. As we rode down a straightaway surrounded on either side by cornfields, Ralph told me that this was his meditation time. This was freedom to him, and I knew what he meant by the sixth and seventh day being his to do what he pleased.

JO
EDITOR, *HARLEY WOMEN* MAGAZINE

Jo was racing cars when she was a teenager. Her boyfriend picked her up one night and took her for her first ride on a bike. She was scared to death riding on the back, so she tried riding it herself. She wasn't interested at all in learning how to ride. Her boyfriend tried teaching her on a tankshift Panhead, which Jo said was really hard to learn on let alone ride on. She hated it. Jo tried riding a small bike, said it was really easy to handle and that was it. She's been hooked ever since.

That was twenty-three years ago. In that time she's owned eight bikes, one Triumph and seven Harleys after that. Jo started the second chapter of Women in the Wind in the Chicago area, a women's motorcycle club. They came out with a two-page newsletter and the women went nuts over it. Jo realized women were hungry for something that they could read and identify with as a woman motorcyclist or enthusiast. That's how *Harley Women* magazine began. After the second issue more material was submitted, and now the magazine is published bimonthly and runs up to seventy-two pages. *Harley Women* magazine has subscribers all over the states and in nineteen other countries.

Jo says the biggest comment she gets from her female readers is that when they get their new issue, they end up hiding it so they can read it before their old man does. It's become the first Harley family magazine that's out.

"I started riding in '67. There were very few women on bikes then. It's just started to snowball. And men are accepting it more. I had a few times when it was not accepted. I've had some hassles with men that ride who do not think I belonged on the front, that I belonged on the back. But I think a lot of men today realize when you're riding a bike it's a lot more fun to ride a bike solo than it is to have somebody on the back.

"We've been at events and men have come up to us dragging their old ladies by the arm saying 'here, these women ride, talk to them.' They're trying to encourage them to ride their own bikes. They've bought our magazine to try to get their wife or girlfriend more interested in motorcycling. Either to ride their own bike or just ride as a passenger. But it's becoming more accepted. The men of the nineties don't seem so intimidated as back in the sixties or early seventies. Their egos don't seem to be hurt as much when they see a woman can handle a Harley-Davidson as well as they can. I was

JO

*988 Harley-Davidson Heritage softail,
1340 cc, Screamin' Eagle cam,
carburetor, and module*

taught to ride by men and I rode mainly with men the first twenty years I was riding. Now I've got a lot of girlfriends who are riding. If you see a pack of bikes go by at Sturgis, there's usually a woman in there. On a bigger bike. It's growing rapidly. Anybody that is interested at all should take a motorcycle safety course. It's the best way to learn how to ride. I wish they had had them when I was learning how to ride. Life is too short. Get out there and try it. If you like it, you've added something to your life. Besides, girls on bikes attract a lot of attention from men and you can pick up guys, too. But that's not why I do it."

ON BEING A GOOD BITCH

There's a lot that goes into being a good bitch, whether you're the chick on the back or you have your own bike. Some women really get into riding on the back seat, being able to look around and hang on to the guy driving. Being someone's bitch, or old lady, can give you a feeling of power and the opportunity to navigate. To some, taking care of your old man—whether it's your husband, boyfriend, or just a friend—that's what being a good bitch is all about. Some women would never dream of jumping on the back of a bike other than their old man's. Others ride with a lot of different guys because they like to ride. But, as a woman, you have to be careful who you ride with, sometimes because of the bike, and sometimes because of the bike's owner.

There are a lot of great bros who will take you for a putt just because they know you love to ride and that's it. Other guys think that just because you go for a ride you want to fuck them. Then there's the women who are prisoners, either by choice or by chance; and where clubs are concerned, they can become trapped and at the mercy of any member's whims. This can occur even when clubs are not involved.

One woman, who is not affiliated with a club but has seen a lot in her life, described it this way: "Some women are mammas and some aren't. If you're around these people enough you know. You can tell the women that are hard at heart and the women that just ride. Some women ride because they like to ride. Others are prisoners. They don't really want to be that way. They feel they're safe. Wearing a property patch makes them feel like they belong. They prove it to their old man so they stay for who knows how long. For my old man I'd bend over backwards, but I wouldn't wear 'Property Of.' Some people are lucky and can break away. Some women can't, especially with clubs."

There are biker men who tend to have the same opinions regarding these women and feel the women that become victims lack common sense and initially don't realize what they are getting themselves into.

There are women that are turned on by the biker image. They want to see it and experience it firsthand, and that's where the trouble starts. Old ladies tend to be dedicated to their men and in many cases have a lot more on the ball than their old man.

One guy who's been riding for over thirty years had a few things to say about biker women: "Some old ladies are wives. Some old

SHORT

ladies are steady girlfriends. Some are just hang-arounds, and some old ladies are just street trash. If a guy takes a hankerin' to street trash and he puts his patch on her, then she's an old lady. A lot of bikers are true to their old ladies, even if they screw around with other women. No matter what he does he goes back to the old lady. She's the mother of his kids, even though some of these guys have two, three, or four old ladies—sometimes all over the country. And they usually support all of them. They're not just fluffs. A fluff is just any chickey that comes around, some little hard body they meet up with, and that's a one-night stand, that's it. And if he's tired of her or she bitches too much, he passes her on to somebody else. They see a situation that they think is glamorous. Once these guys get started drinking and whatever else they may be doing, they may retire to a tent, whoever this guy is that brought some girl with him. When everybody hears what's going on, they'll go look in the tent. Or they may all go skinny dipping. And that might be a girl's big mistake. You don't walk around without a club in your hand when your in a den of wolves. And it's true when you're with a bunch of bikers. You've gotta cover your ass, watch your back. One beer leads to two beers, to three beers, and it's a four-beer broad.

And now she's had eight. Now she's had ten. And now a band starts playin'. And she's going to give them all a little look. She's going to dance around or there'll be a 'show your titties' sign.

These guys already know she's got a certain amount of freedom about herself and they're going to see how far it goes. If you get enough drunken people around, it's going to get out of hand. It goes further than she thinks it's going to go. If they rape some broad at a party, they have to look at the fact that they may get caught. But who's gonna testify?"

"Property of," mammas, prisoners, or whatever you care to call it is a small percentage of women motorcycle enthusiasts. A woman can hang out with bikers because she likes the feeling of the brotherhood.

Rusty, the real mother portrayed by Cher in the movie *Mask*, feels this way about bikers and explains why she has hung out with them all her life: "Maybe a woman never had any brothers and just wants to open up her heart to the bond of love that these brothers can offer and share. I never had any brothers, and I think that's why I started hanging around with bikers. Women like me are brothers also. They choose to be with them because of the love and brotherhood that is found there. I would never wear a property patch and the club would tell me that I had to wear my boyfriend's patch and I refused. I said if I ever wore a patch it would say 'Property of the Universe.'"

There are women who choose to be victims. They seem to feel the need to be at someone's mercy, saying they are trapped in their way of life. This may be selling drugs or being involved in prostitution where the profits go to the old man or in some cases a club itself. But these women make the choices themselves and may say they are trapped and victimized. But it is their choice and there is a way out. If a woman can come to terms with being her own person and in touch with who she is and her self-worth, she can break free or never feel victimized in her own mind.

Most women that ride are their own person. Society has put the label on them as being a piece of property of the guy they ride with. They are in actuality people with feelings of their own and a say in what goes on. Just because they ride on the back of a bike doesn't necessarily make them subservient to the guy driving it. It's the onlooker in the society outside the biker community that sees it that way, reading into what it is they have seen on television and in movies as the image of the biker woman. More women are riding their own

STEF

bikes, and for the most part the guys that ride are accepting of them and willing to help. But a woman doesn't need to have her own bike to feel this strength. A woman can be her own person on the back of a bike, too. It's a feeling from within of self-worth, and unless a woman has the inner strength of these convictions of independence, she will be victimized because she chooses to be so.

The role of woman as victim still occurs, but for the most part, women and motorcycles and how they relate to each other holds great respect among those who love to ride. However, there will always be the element of violence, pain, and torture some women endure, as long as they allow it. Some of these women thrive on it or maybe just think it's the way they have to be.

"If you get caught up in it, you get caught up in it. If you got an old man that's not workin', just bikin' and partyin', it's a pretty rough life for his old lady. But, it's just common sense."

Attitudes regarding the role of men and women vary with individuals or a couple's relationship. Every guy that rides has his own idea of what makes a good old lady.

Mike, who is happily married and a genuinely caring guy, feels the perfect old lady is one who's willing to take the man's shit: "Some

BRAT

of us dish out a lot of it. For instance, if I want to go somewhere with just the guys, you know, for a weekend or something, it's OK. And that's good. When my wife met me she thought I was disgusting. And I said, 'If she thinks I'm disgusting, to hell with her.' But she got to know me and one thing led to another. Before you know it, we're sitting on the steps at my house, I'm reading a book, and she's poppin' the blackheads on my back. We were in love from then on. She knew who I was and what I was and she fell in love with that person."

Spider Leggs considers herself a truly good bitch, with no insecurities regarding her abilities as a woman or a person, taking care of both her old man and his bike. She says she loves to keep the bike clean and that her old man doesn't take care of it anymore, she does: "I clean the bike and polish it. Yeah, I'm a good bitch. I taped off his tanks for him and painted 'em. I help him wrench on it cuz I love workin' on machines. I don't mind gettin' greasy."

In return for being a good bitch, the men take care of the women. You're always around friends and if anything did go down the men are always there to protect the women. Someone's always watching or listening in case you need help. But because the women are "taken

PRESHUS

care of" it sometimes puts them in a position of going along with what the guy wants. The men like to be seen as being in control. Marti, Bear's old lady, has been riding on the back seat for years. She adores Bear, but realizes how he is and always will be.

Marti has seen a lot of interaction between men and women through the years riding with Bear and knows how these guys like to maintain a certain sense of independence: "You can't get them to ever give you an answer. They can't commit. You never really have them. You just have to accept it. That's the way it is. You can't tell them anything. They're gonna do what they want no matter what. Let the old man have the air in his hair even if you're not there, cuz he'll be back and there'll be other days to have the breeze in your hair, too."

Most men that ride are faithful to their old lady, but that's usually when she too likes to ride and be with him, doing what he likes to do. If she's interested, that's great. If not, tough luck for her because he'll be out there telling women his wife doesn't understand him and he'll be looking for a girlfriend. To a lot of these guys, their bike is everything. If his old lady wants to ride he can be devoted and loyal. If she doesn't understand or doesn't want to participate, then it's "fuck you, I'll go by myself."

For the most part, bikers that have been riding for years think that it's great that more women than ever before are riding their own bikes. But some men feel threatened by a woman that rides a motorcycle; they feel that only a man, as one guy put it, can "handle the iron steed." There are a lot of men that think of their bike as their woman, their lover. This is another form of a good bitch, the bitch being the bike itself.

This is how Swanny feels about his bike: "What I do with my bike is as important as any woman. I'm as close to my motorcycle as I will be to any woman. If the bike screws up and lets you down it's either because it failed mechanically due to something you have no control over, or you didn't keep up with it mechanically. But a woman's relationship with you can fail at any time. And it could be that you had nothing to do with it at all. The only freedom you allow yourself outside the relationship is your bike. And she'll still screw you around. And the bike becomes a personal thing—'that's my bitch, my baby.' And to most guys it's true. That's why you see a lot of guys, especially among the Harley riders and the hardcore riders and the 1%ers and even the old hardcore non-1%ers, they keep ridin' the same bike for years. They do it cuz they're attached to it. It's like a marriage. It's like a lover. If the lover's good to you, you'll keep it. If the lover's shitty to you, you get rid of it. Same with a bike.

"Women a lot of times can't understand that. They can't understand what it's like to get out and really feel the wind in your face. It's not the same as a passenger as when you swing your leg over and feel the engine throb between your legs. And it isn't a giant vibrator. It's more than that. It's probably the feeling people years ago got when they rode powerful horses. It makes you feel good. It feels like you can go anywhere you want to go.

"Sometimes you fall asleep or fuck up or don't pay enough attention or some of the elements get beyond your control. The bike itself generally takes care of you. You'll feel feelings that you're not going to feel anywhere else. When a woman starts to ride, then she starts to feel it, too. She feels the wind in her face. She feels the power of the bike. The freedom.

"Feeling the wind in your face, letting the wind fall through your hair, letting the rain fall in your face, your fingers so goddamn cold you can hardly hold them on the grips, it still keeps you alive and

JENI

makes you know why you're alive and why you like being alive. It gives you speed. It gives you power. It gives you anything you want it to give you. It's just you and the bike. On a motorcycle, you feel it with your whole body. And when you love those feelings and understand them, it behooves a man that rides a motorcycle to want the woman he's with to get the same feeling cuz then she understands what he's feeling and why he feels this way about his bike and the freedom that he has from riding. And once she starts riding, she can sympathize and empathize with what he's doing. There's nothing that will soothe the savage beast in a man like a nice long ride. No matter how angry or pissed off you are. No matter how much you feel the world is shittin' all over you. You go out for a ride, and when you come back, it's OK."

Being a good bitch is more than just looking good and wiping the bugs off the windshield and chrome. A woman must respect the bond between a guy and his bike. Or the bond that she has with her own bike. Either way, the respect is necessary. You never know when that bike will save your life.

BIG DADDY'S WEDDING

Big Daddy and Cathy were married on the thirteenth of January in a rural courthouse at 9:30 in the morning. The wedding party met at Offie's Tap for screwdrivers before departing for the ceremony. Cathy rode with Marlene in her truck; on the way Marlene told her she had one last chance to bail out and not go through with it. The bride and groom wore leather and so did all the witnesses. Cathy's knees were shaking under her leather miniskirt. Marlene was the matron of honor; she wanted her picture taken with the judge in case she ever found herself in traffic court.

After the ceremony the wedding party drove to the 2nd Chance Saloon for cocktails. The bride and groom traveled in separate vehicles. Big Daddy had a bottle of cheap champagne that everyone guzzled. Marlene said she gave the marriage three weeks. The reception was the next day at the Country Junction, a country-western dancehall surrounded by farm fields. By eleven A.M. everyone was smashed. The bride said she made the potato salad and mostaccioli at two in

the morning. The menu consisted of foods high in calories, carbohydrates, and cholesterol and was served in large heated crocks. Big Daddy and Cathy were wearing the same outfits that they were wearing the day before. They both appeared exuberant and blissful.

Bikers from all of the surrounding areas were in attendance. When Big Daddy and Cathy cut the cake, Big Daddy took a piece and smeared it in his bride's face. Cathy did the same to Big Daddy, who continued to smoke his Pall Mall through the cake on his face and hands.

One month later I ran into Marlene and Jack in their tavern. Marlene said, "Did you hear?"

"Hear what?" I responded.

"Oh, she hasn't heard," Marlene said as the group next to us at the bar turned to listen. "Big Daddy and Cathy are getting an annulment.

"I told you three weeks and I was right. Didn't I say three weeks?"

But everyone agreed it was a great party.

OLD LADIES

"Sometimes guys stay with their old ladies because of the ingrown fear that some of them know too much. Sometimes it's because the old lady has put up with their shit for a long time and they were true blue to them. You'll find that most of them come from broken homes or not very stable homes. Bikers I'm talking about. So when they find a woman that's stayed loyal to them, that means something. I know bikers that have left their old ladies, ten, twelve years ago, gone on to other women and other women after that. Yet they still have a fondness for the original old ladies, the ones that were with them when they were first being challenged by the things that were goin' down in the clubs and the things they were doing. They stuck with them for that period of time and they still have a fondness for them. So they're stuck with them. They've gone on to other women and gone back to their old ladies. I know some that have been married twenty or thirty years and have stuck with them. Because the old lady has stuck with him. She's raised their kids and done a pretty good job. But if a woman hangs with a club, she knows a lot, and she better keep her trap shut." —Anonymous

YVETTE & DETROIT

BEAR & MARTI

MIKE & BETTY

SPIDER & CHERI

LEANN & SPIDER

STEF & CHEAKS

SPIDER LEGGS

Spider Leggs lives with her old man Too Tall in a house that once belonged to her mother. She started riding motorcycles when she was six years old, on dirt bikes and stuff. She got her first Harley when she was sixteen, a chopper with a springer front end; a 70-inch converted to a 72-inch Sportster.

That's how she got the name Spider Leggs. She'd be riding her chopper and people would tell her she looked like a spider in a web, because her legs are so long. Spider Leggs thinks there's something real special about American bikes. She rode an Indian once and thought it was great. Now she rides on the back seat with Too Tall.

Before they went on their first date, she told him "I'm not gonna fuck you, I ain't gonna go out with you, I ain't gonna kiss ya, I ain't gonna date ya." Too Tall told her he didn't like sluts and they've been together ever since.

Spider Leggs says bikers look upon their bikes as children. She thinks that bikers are a lot more mellow than fifteen years ago, when more people were into being renegades. She says there was a lot of rivalry, showing off, and doing mean things—just being an asshole as much as you could. But now that she has a child she says it's changed the way she feels about things. She tries not to be so wild,

SPIDER LEGGS

but still carries a bag of rice with her to give people on riceburners a hard time.

"I like working on bikes. I think if you've got a Harley-Davidson, an Indian, or even a Triumph, it's great because they're gorgeous. They ride well, and they have great balance. They may not be first off the line, but I'm not into speed. They're comfortable, it feels good havin' that VOOM with you and we've got them underwater pipes. I take a lot of pride in the bike. I like the prestige. I like the attitude cuz I've always had it. People say 'have the attitude, you're supposed to look cool on a bike' and I say I'm havin' fun. If I want to sit there with my shit-eating grin, I don't care if I get bugs in my teeth.

"Bikers are down-to-earth. They've got good humor and dry humor. You can dryly insult somebody and they don't get insulted. They know it's a joke. You can play on somebody's bad points or good points and they don't get insulted. This guy would pour beer down the back of my pants. So I put grease in his kick and he went flyin'. He did get pissed. Like I said, if you do anything to their bike, it's their baby, it's their kid. But it sure was fun gettin' even."

TOO TALL

Tattoo design by Spider Leggs.

MARLENE

Marlene has owned Offie's Tap with her old man Jack for fourteen years. When Marlene took over the bar she abolished club colors and laid down a few rules. Offie's is a bar where anyone can sit down and relax. Her clientele are considered family and her bar is a place where problems disappear and characters aren't questioned. Marlene tends bar Sunday afternoons and socializes with her patrons the rest of the time. Club colors are still not allowed except when Marlene is working, and then it's very rare.

Marlene is a self-proclaimed midwife, priest, mother, and sister. She loves Jack Daniels, her jukebox, and the Milwaukee Vibrator. "When these guys finally get on a bike they realize what freedom is. That's what Harley is all about—just them and a bike. That's why a bike is referred to as a she. Something they can really take pride in and be one with. It's a sense of relaxation and freedom. No matter how you feel when you enter my bar, in five minutes you're one of a feeling that is genuine."

MARLENE

OFFIE'S TAP

Offie's Tap is more a feeling than a place one can describe. The people that frequent this tavern do so because of the people they'll see there. When you walk through the beat-up, weathered door someone will greet you, regardless of whether you've ever been there before. When Marlene's bartending on Sunday afternoons, everybody gets a greeting. "Get out of here, we don't want any biker trash in here." If you say you're going out for a ride with someone she'll jokingly call you a slut. You sit down and your beer is in front of you before you ask for it. Then everybody tells you what happened the night before and how "you should have been there."

Offie's Tap at night casts an amber tone on everything. The light from the beer signs is deflected and diffused by the nicotine-stained walls. The seedy side takes over, as there isn't any afternoon sunlight streaming through the windows. The jukebox is a lot louder, the conversation turns into boisterous laughter, and the groups are more tightly knit. Some drink alone. Some drink alone and look for an argument. When fights occur, Marlene and Jack merely observe at first, waiting to see if whatever it is will be resolved before taking any action. If beer bottles or glasses are broken, Marlene gets the broom and dustpan, her silence conveying her disgust to the culprits

BUFFALO

involved. All she usually has to say is we're all family here, and have been for twenty-five years.

It truly is like family at Offie's. Everybody understands the behavior of particular individuals and takes it, overlooks it, or ignores it. Everyone's got a story and it's not questioned. But if a newcomer tries to start trouble, there are people there that will teach  him a lesson on interfering with the clan.

You go to Offie's to feel like you belong. A lot of the patrons are connected historically. Many are children of a former generation of Offie's regulars. The forefathers still work on the bikes, come in for their beers, flirt with the girls, and fall asleep in their chairs and it's accepted.

No one's behavior is made public spectacle unless he or she chooses otherwise. The people look out for each other. Your friends keep you in check. They make sure over and over again that everything's OK. If you don't feel like drinking and have a Pepsi, it's nobody's business but your own. There's always a friend there, a

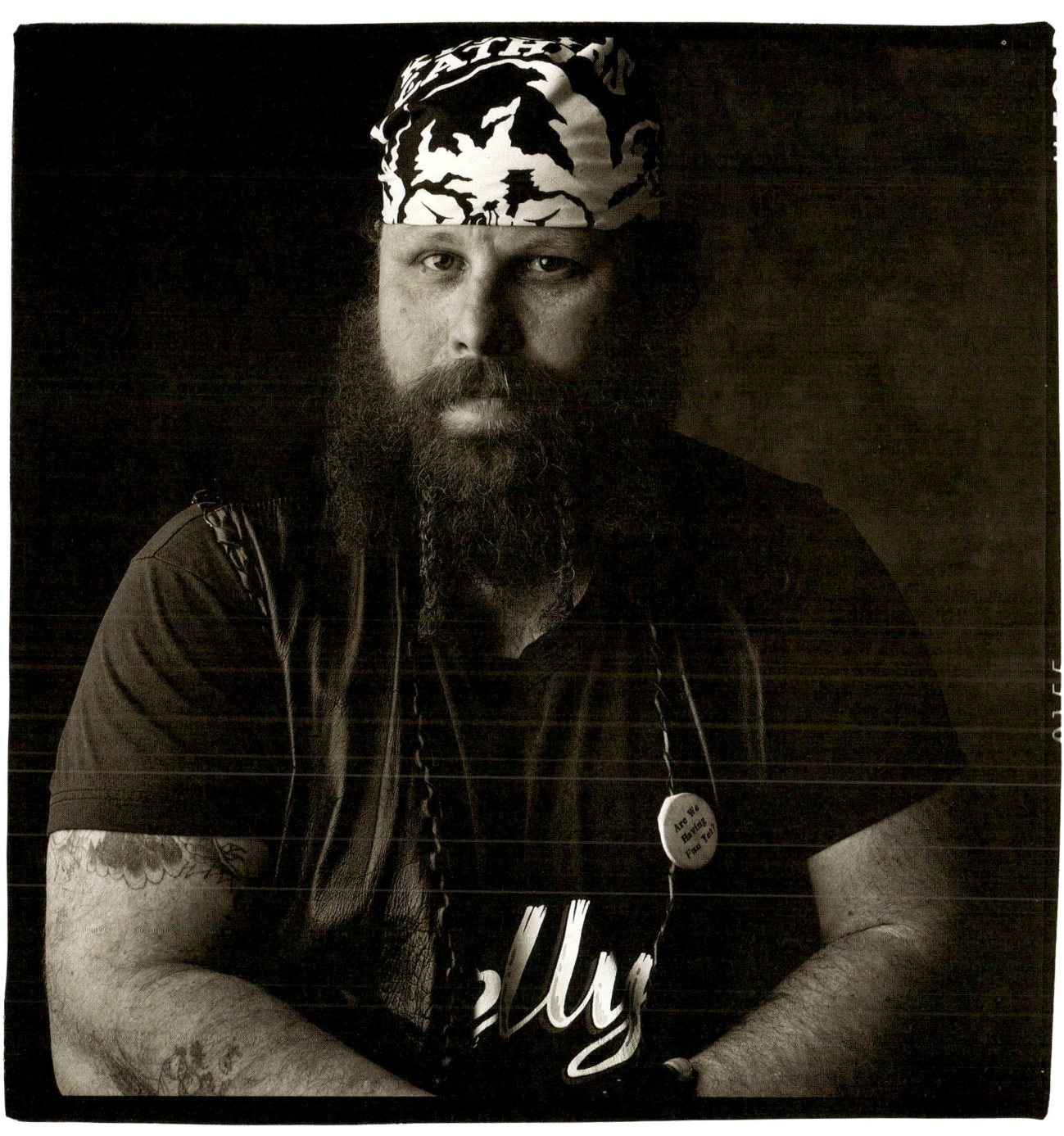

BIG RICH

ride on a Harley, a pool game for a beer, or a casual conversation with one of the regulars.

A lot of the patrons live only a few blocks away or across the street. Others travel miles. On a Sunday afternoon in the summer, bikes can be seen lined up all around the corner. No club colors or attitudes. Everyone gets along or you get out. Logic prevails and right and wrong rules. If somebody gets out of hand, they know it immediately and it's taken care of.

Offie's is located on Main Street in a small town surrounded by farmland. There's a Harley emblem on the door, and a Blatz sign outside, even though Offie's doesn't serve Blatz anymore. Offie's has been there for forty years and has remained virtually the same. There are oil stains on the sidewalk even in  the dead of winter. When spring is on the verge of arrival, the energy level surges, and spills outside. All the regulars are in and out, talking about bikes and where they're going on their first run of the season. The most excitement is to be found during this time of year

BEAR

and good moods run rampant. You see people you haven't seen since the previous summer. There's not enough time in an afternoon to get it all in. They've all got a sunburned noses and stories about traveling and what went wrong and right with their bikes.

A lot of the bikes have been down over the winter, and look like brand new pieces of fine craftsmanship to be adored. These people are proud, and this is their opportunity to show it. History through the oral tradition is gospel at Offie's, as the patrons come and go, resurface, and then disappear again.

You generally know what day and time to run into someone in particular. Some of the patrons bring their kids along to the bar every time they bring themselves in. The kids run around the bar, taking everyone on as their family. But this can turn into hours of drinking, and a lonely kid sitting on a barstool with a troubled look on his face. Marlene finally got disgusted and put up a sign "No Children After 9:00 P.M." When the bar is closed on holidays, such as Easter Sunday and Christmas, Marlene and Jack usually open their home to the regulars that don't have families to be with. They've got a huge bar in the basement, and refer to it as "Offie's West."

Marlene closed the bar one Saturday night in honor of Jack's

JIMBO

birthday. A big party was held at Marlene and Jack's that night. Unlimited cases of beer were consumed, and a quarter slot machine was used to fund such future events. The party ran between the yard and the basement, and shots of Jack Daniels were a must. There was no ventilation in the basement, and a blue fog of cigarette smoke permeated the air. The men were in their uniforms: jeans, black Harley T-shirts with colorful silk-screened pictures on the front. Most of these men wore black leather vests that were decorated with pins and patches from places and events. Keys and wallets were attached to their belts with chrome chains. The women were in their Saturday night attire, a little more makeup than usual, and new blue jeans.

Marlene was holding court at the bar and Jack was watching soft porn on cable television, asking the girls sitting around the bar to show him their tits.

One notorious troublemaker was roaming the crowd, already loud and obnoxious and on the verge of being considered unruly. There was definitely a faction of dislike among the crowd regarding this person. He had an alcohol-bloated face and a smashed-in nose that told a history of opening his mouth when he shouldn't have.

WOODY

The troublemaker doesn't ride a motorcycle and is constantly bumming rides and threatening suicide. He once intentionally cut his hand in Offie's and stated he was a hemophiliac and that someone better call an ambulance. Marlene gave him a towel and told him to clean up the mess that was all over the bar and men's room.

It was now 3:00 A.M. at Jack's birthday party. The crowd was still lively. There was one guy that sat in the same place the entire evening, and he was now staring blankly into space. A young blond guy told me how the biker thing was a bond, a brotherhood. He emphasized the idea of family, and how he felt welcome among these people, that things would always be taken care of.

He said that when he was six years old he nearly drowned in a northern Illinois lake and was saved by a guy he knew rode a Harley-Davidson. "The guy slapped me around a little to bring me back to life. Then he gave me a ride home. It was then that I knew I would be into motorcycles and this way of life."

There was a sudden commotion at the bar and the troublemaker with the smashed in nose was being dragged up the stairs by one of the bros. Everyone stopped to listen to the slamming around upstairs. There was a crash as the troublemaker fell through the

CHEAKS

screen door leading outside, destroying it.

Marlene and Jack remained in the basement, seemingly calm as their home appeared to be torn apart. The troublemaker returned to the basement, making his way around the bar explaining his version of what had happened. Most everyone seemed uninterested in his efforts to redeem himself, which he accompanied with nervous laughter. The guy bartending seemed to be excited and was screaming into everyone's face. His face would become very red as he yelled,

and the veins in his neck bulged. He was wearing a baseball cap that said "Born Wild" and his eyes looked like they were out of focus. His screaming gibberish was so alcohol induced it ceased to sound like anything recognizable, but more of a redneck slang. The party finally waned and broke up around sunrise.

Offie's Tap is a feeling of being home. The people go there because they feel comfortable. There's an ambience that you just can't put your finger on. Even though there are a few assholes who try to

TOOTSIE & MERLE

ruin things for everyone else, those cases are rare. It's usually the ones that shouldn't be there that try to make trouble. Like Marlene says, "It's one thing for one of us to make fun of each other. But if somebody comes in here and just decides to start cuttin' everybody down, that's not right." It's happened, and there will be a crowd ready to back you up. A lot of places you have to watch your back. Here you never have to worry about anything but having a good time and listening for the sound of loud pipes pulling up outside.

BUTCH

LU & MARLENE

RICK ON STURGIS

"When I first started going to Sturgis, it was a lot less commercial. It was more about bike shows and races, but I've been going for ten years and haven't been to a race yet. I take it back, I went to the drag strip a few times. The first time I went to Sturgis I went

with Ronny and Randy—the twins, Marti, Dave, and Ed V. The first year I went I had a wheel bearing go out on me on the tollway. And those guys said well we'll stop for gas and leave somebody on the ramp and you can catch up. And I limped down 25 to Elgin and got the wheel bearing fixed. It took about an hour and a half. I told the guy it was a left-hand thread and he was tightening it all the time he was trying to get it off. So I was riding alone the first day. I rode 600 miles by myself in about twelve hours. And the guys had trouble in LaCrosse that I didn't know about. One of the guys had his oil lines hooked up wrong and he was spewin' oil all over and he seized the bottom end in LaCrosse.

"They found a shop and the guy told him to start the bike up if he could. He got it goin' about two or three times after it cooled down for a short period of time. And the guy said 'where are you goin' on this bike?' and he said 'Sturgis.' And he said 'not this year.' So those guys were behind me and I made it all the way to Sioux Falls. That's where I met Ed Vincent. Ed was a leather guy. He was a Vietnam vet and he went haywire. Last I heard he was in some mental institution someplace. But he was a real cool guy. When you're ridin' by yourself, you kinda set a pace. And other people that are settin' that pace, you keep runnin' into 'em at gas stops and rest stops.

"Ed wore a leather cowboy hat and had this crazy windshield and he had leather tank covers. You know, wild tooled leather. And he had his leather chaps and leather vest. And every time I saw this guy he'd look at me and smile and wave. Then I wouldn't see him again until I stopped for gas and I got back on the road and he'd be passin' me again. Finally we hooked up in the KOA of Sioux Falls and got to talkin' about who we're waitin' for and he's waitin' for the same guys I'm waitin' for. He's waitin' for Ronny and Randy. They know each other and I'm thinkin' 'man, what a small world.' After that, we hooked up the next day and it rained—pretty much from Sioux Falls to Wall. And in Wall we stopped and had a bite to eat, some beers, and then we all rode down to Sturgis.

"My partner Dave, it was his first time too, he had problems with his primary chain. So we had to leave the bike at the dealer in Rapid City, cuz he took it apart and he couldn't get it back together again before the dealer closed, so we figured we'll just put the bike inside and lock it up for the night. Then he rode on the buddy seat with me into Sturgis. We went to City Park. That's where we camped. They've closed it for camping now. It was the camp from hell. I was so tired I just passed out on the ground next to my bike. The other guys set up their tents and went into town for some beers and it got dark and when I woke up, all these other bikers from Tennessee and Kentucky, all these hillbilly fuckheads, are all around our tents. So about that time, some crazy guy ridin' around naked through the campground comes wheelin' around the corner and he missed the path and went slidin' through the grass right through a guy's tent. And that guy had just got out of that tent no more than ten seconds before that. I swear to God. If he had been in that tent, he probably would've got killed. And as the bike slid into the tent and stopped, the nylon started burning. And the bike burned. And this was my introduction to Sturgis. And you get all these guys runnin' over there throwin' dirt on the bike. And in the morning, the bike's still layin' there. But all night long you hear guns goin' off. I'm not talkin' one shot here, one shot there. I'm talkin' boom boom boom boom. And you could hear the fuckin' bullets whistling through the trees. I wished I had a shovel to dig a foxhole.

"In the morning, we decided we were all going to go somewhere else to camp. In '81, the last year they had camping at City Park, it turned into such a zoo that cops wouldn't even go in. You'd come through the gate and you'd have your wristband on and that's the last you saw of any organized control. Once you got inside, it was up for grabs. We saw guys bring their old ladies in on the back of the bike, get surrounded by the throng chanting 'show your tits,' and if they didn't show their tits, if the crowd was drunk enough and it was dark enough, there was a good chance she'd get ripped off the bike and taken off to wherever. That was the last year they had camping at City Park. The johns got so full of shit that the guys who thought they were the acting camp directors decided that for sanitary reasons they'd just burn them down. That's when the city fathers decided there'd be no more camping at City Park."

SWANNY

"I've been riding since I was fourteen. This is my thirty-third year. I've had a montage of bikes. I hope to be riding when I'm sixty-five. I make my living off of bikes. My feeling is bikes. I'm an artist. But I just paint on a different canvas, that's all. My motorcycles enhance my life. They make it worth living. They've got me through hard times a lot easier than not having a motorcycle."

SWANNY

HOWARD

JEFF
CO-OWNER, BIKER'S CHOICE, GLENVIEW, ILLINOIS

ON THE GOOD OLD DAYS

"My dad rode with the Windy City Motorcycle Club before the Second World War, a 1936 61 Knucklehead to hill climbs. There used to be a lot of hill climbs held out by Carey. Before the Second World War, if you rode out to Carey, that was a day's ride there and back. They didn't have the kind of highways you see today and streets were real narrow. Anyway, he rode before the war and always told stories about his motorcycling days. And then when I got to be gettin' close enough to be gettin' a driver's license, I was workin' in a gas station for my uncle in the city. So I told the old man I wanted a bike. I wanted something small. I was still in high school. We were glad to get anything we could get. The first bike I had was a 400 cc Norton Electra. I had that for awhile and then I got a 750 Matchless, then a Sportster, and then the Harley that I have now. But I had other bikes along the way. I was workin' in the Triumph shop at Midwest Triumph on Cicero Avenue. And when you work sixty hours a week in a motorcycle shop, the last thing you want to do is maintenance on your own bike. So I got a Yamaha.

JEFF

1964 FLH Police Special

That Harley, even though it's been a good reliable bike, it's very maintenance-oriented.

"Back in the old days, it was a lot different than it is now, for a lot of different reasons. Prior to all the Hondas and jap bikes comin' in, all bikers were considered bad guys. Whether you were or you weren't, it didn't make any difference. That was just the image you portrayed, regardless. All the bigger clubs were outlaw-style clubs. So people would see big groups of a club and they got a lot of publicity.

"There was the movie *Easy Rider* that came out in '69, so you can still see then in '69 how they were still portrayin' bikers as bein' a bunch of drunks and drug addicts. It was just the way that people thought about bikers. Generally you didn't get too much hassle. I rode with a club some. I would go on runs with a club, cuz I was too young to join the club, but as a guest I got to go with 'em. So we'd walk into a bar, get a beer, sit in a corner, shut up, and don't cause any problems. And nobody will hassle ya. They never really gave anybody any trouble. Unless somebody gave them trouble.

"The cops were constantly after ya. Because ya had loud pipes and stuff and there wasn't much traffic around and as soon as you rolled it on they heard ya. The cops had an attitude in those days. Tryin' to be assholes to bikers. There was no question about that. They tried to make life as miserable as they could. That took some of the fun out of ridin'.

"Every Wednesday night there were short track races at Sante Fe. That was a big thing to go to. It was always a place to go at the time. There were a lot of races and things around in those days that aren't around anymore. A couple big races every year out at Meadowdale. Any kind of race was an excuse for everybody to get together and go for a ride. The thing that made biking better later on once Harley really got on their feet and got HOG clubs goin' is that it gave bikers a place to go and a purpose to ride. Because a lot of people didn't have anyone to ride with. That was one of the reasons that bikes started to drop off. I think HOG started somewhere around '83. Before that, people either belonged to outlaw-style bike clubs or moped around with their buddies. That's why clubs got to be as strong as they did. It was camaraderie.

"Part of the reason to ride with somebody was when the bikes were unreliable, if you were stuck on the side of the road by yourself it wasn't very much fun. If you had a couple of your buddies with ya, you at least didn't have to walk home or you had somebody to run and get parts or run and get a sixpack while you were fixin' it. Guys would ride in large groups because they'd be a lot more noticeable on the street than one or two guys.

"A lot of times you just went for a ride anywhere you wanted to go just for the hell of it. You didn't need too much of an excuse on a nice summer night. From the early sixties, when I first got started there weren't wanna-be bikers like there are now. Now people can go out and buy a Harley and they're immediately a Harley rider. Anybody who's got a decent job and can make payments can own a Harley. In those days it wasn't like that. Most of the guys worked their butts off at whatever job they were doin' and their bike was a second kind of thing. They made parts. If they needed a sissy bar they bent one up out of concrete reinforcements and put it on their bike. If they painted it, they did it with a spray can. The average biker was not a wealthy guy by any means. He had to scrounge. He had to learn to work on his own bike. He couldn't afford to take it in and pay somebody to have it fixed. Now people ride 'em up to the door and say 'hey, here's my bike, fix it, and I'm gone.' Or they say 'here's a basket of parts, I want to ride out of here on a chopper.'

"Most of 'em don't know the front end of the bike from the back. We learned to be bikers by payin' our dues. You went out and bought whatever you could afford and ya rode it, and if it broke, you either fixed it or read a book and found out how to fix it. Or asked someone or saved your money and eventually went somewhere and had just one item fixed. If you needed a valve job, you had it done. You didn't go in and say 'here's five thousand dollars, build me a motorcycle.'

"Chrome wasn't in like it is now. Guys wanted things chromed on bikes, there's no doubt about it. But nowadays, any part they can buy chromed that they can bolt on they do. It seems like the more chrome they have on their bike they feel like a dyed-in-the-wool hardcore biker. A good example is guys that went to Sturgis and trailered their bikes. The whole idea of Sturgis is not to go out there and get drunk and party. The reason you did things like that years ago was to prove that you could make it there and back on your bike. Regardless of what you had there was no way you were going to trailer your bike out there. That just didn't happen. And everybody went together and they left together and they got back together. If a guy broke down, everybody stayed around to help him fix it. If one guy never worked on his bike and was breakin' down constantly, the other guys would say, 'look pal, you're not ridin' with us cuz you don't take the time to work on your bike. Either fix it and get it right or you're not welcome to come with us.'

"Years ago, bikers knew what they wanted. And they came in and told you what they wanted, not what can I put on my bike to make it go faster. Nobody was an expert from the beginning. There were guys around then just like there is now that knew what the hot setup was, but it was just a different attitude. If you were a young punk and you didn't know nothin' about a bike and you went up to a biker that you knew was older than you and you asked him a question, they were generally helpful. There wasn't that attitude 'oh, I got a secret here.'

"Now they have more money. They buy anything and everything they can whether they need it or not. Just cuz it's pretty. Its like a fashion show. Guys didn't have money for that kind of stuff years ago. That's just the way it was. A typical chopper of the day is a good example. A chopper was just a stock Harley with the big fenders taken off. What they used to use to make the rear fender was a Continental kit off a Lincoln. And they'd put one of them on the back. Or some guys would take it and put it on the front, they'd put it on backwards.

"Something that really killed club participation was any of the guys that were halfway decent as far as had any kind of sense of responsibility quit ridin' with clubs because it turned out to be a front for prostitution, stealin' bikes, and a lot of that kind of shit. Guys that wanted to ride and didn't want to have the cops harassin' them and gettin' jagged with all the time. They didn't want anything to do with the clubs. It was only the guys that were out of work and didn't want to work and that were drunks and couldn't hold a job and shit like that. They lived in the clubhouse like a bunch of pigs. It's not that a lot of them didn't take a shower because they didn't want to, it's because they didn't have any place to go. They lived like hobos. They slept in a garage on a pile of sleeping bags or whatever. Because they didn't have money to do anything else. The whole image of outlaw bikes changed after *Easy Rider* and Hell's Angels on Wheels because stuff that was goin' on in California, people saw that in the movies. It was the way to be cool. That's why Harley is doin' so well now. Because now it's in to ride a Harley and you can be cool. People will give respect to ya and stuff like that. The popularity of it is acceptable now. It was acceptable years ago, but you were a low-life scumbag if you rode a bike. There's always been all kinds of people. It's just the ones that got the notoriety that were bad guys because they were doin' shit. They'd get half shined up and pull a stunt or somethin'. And the newspapers didn't have anything to write about anyway.

"A lot of guys came back from Nam, they were pissed off, they had a rough way to go over there. They got attitudes or stuff over there and they were glad to be back and they pretty much had the attitude nothing could hurt 'em if they made it through Nam. When they came back, they'd been fightin' a war that really wasn't a war, there was a lot of bullshit goin' on. Guys gettin' blown apart. It had to do something to their mind."